MARVEL

SPIDER-MAN
MUSEUM

THE STORY OF A
COMIC BOOK ICON

A STUDIO PRESS BOOK

First published in the UK in 2022 by Studio Press,
an imprint of Bonnier Books UK,
4th Floor, Victoria House, Bloomsbury Square, London WC1B 4DA
Owned by Bonnier Books,
Sveavägen 56, Stockholm, Sweden

www.bonnierbooks.co.uk

1 3 5 7 9 10 8 6 4 2

ISBN 978-180078-327-0

Written by Ned Hartley
Edited by Saaleh Patel
Designed by Maddox Philpot
Production by Emma Kidd

A CIP catalogue for this book is available from the British Library.
Printed and bound in China

Welcome to the

MARVEL

SPIDER-MAN
MUSEUM

PREFACE

Eleven pages. Stan Lee and Steve Ditko did it in eleven pages!

In 1962, when Spider-Man debuted in the fifteenth issue of an about-to-be-cancelled anthology series called *Amazing Fantasy*, no one could have predicted what was to come. In what are probably the most important eleven pages in Marvel history (if not all of comics), they turned the staid, simplistic idea of super heroes entirely on its head by not only choosing a teenager as their main character (up to that point teens in comics had mostly been sidekicks or comic relief) but by having Peter Parker do something almost unheard of in super hero comics: he made a mistake.

That mistake cost him someone he held dear and led him to a realisation that has come to define not only Spider-Man but all of Marvel's massive library of heroes (you can probably even recite it yourself): "With great power there must also come – great responsibility."

Those eleven pages take you on a darker journey than people sometimes remember and were undoubtedly a shock to the system in those Camelot days. It was just the beginning of a journey of perseverance, one all of literature's heroes must go through if they want to stand the test of time.

Spider-Man is a character born of tragedy who has gone on – in the talented hands of Stan, Steve, John Romita and many, many others – to bring hope, humour and heroism to almost every person who comes across his adventures in comics, novels, records, newspaper strips, TV, cartoons, movies. . . look, it's a *lot* of media, okay? Now, you can see it all in this book! Stan and Steve's creation has gone on to become one of the most recognisable in the world and has inspired generations for 60 years with no signs of stopping.

It started with an eleven-page story, but, as you are about to discover, in eleven pages you can change the world.

Stephen Wacker

Senior Editor, Spider-Man 2007–2014

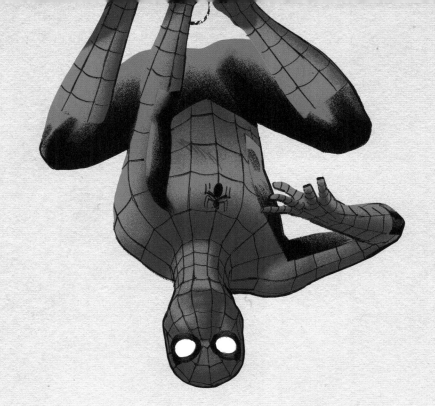

SECTION 1

INCEPTION
& ORIGINS

Creator Spotlight: Stan Lee & Steve Ditko
Along Came a Spider
Timeline

CREATOR SPOTLIGHT:

STAN LEE & STEVE DITKO

In the same way that Spider-Man and Peter Parker are two sides of the same coin, the two creators of Spider-Man were very different but also similar people. Before they created Spider-Man, writer and editor Stan Lee and artist Steve Ditko had worked together for years, but neither expected they would end up creating a character that would define a company, and be an icon for a generation. In many ways Stan and Steve were opposites and complemented each other perfectly. Loud, bombastic Stan was known to jump on the furniture when explaining exciting plot points, while quiet, reserved Steve preferred to stay in his artist studio in Manhattan. As a boy, Steve had always wanted to draw comics, cutting out pages of Prince Valiant from the newspaper, while Stan had dreamed of being a novelist.

Stan started working for Marvel Comics (then Timely Comics) in 1939, first as an assistant but he soon worked his way up to editor, then editor-in-chief. Stan wrote many of the comics, partly to keep costs down, but mainly because he loved writing. Steve's first work for Marvel (which was called Atlas Comics at the time) was in 1956 on *Journey Into Mystery #33*, in a story called "There'll Be Some Changes Made", which features the brilliantly textured, brooding artwork that would come to define his style. Steve and Stan worked together on a range of comics, including *Strange Tales*, *Amazing Adventures*, *Tales to Astonish* and *Amazing Adult Fantasy*. Steve specialised in snappy, four- or five-page science fiction stories, often with a smart twist ending.

Stan, a brash New Yorker, seemed very different to Steve, a boy from a small town in

Pennsylvania, and yet both of these elements came together to form Spider-Man. Years later, Stan would say about Steve, "One of the things about doing Spidey that was the most fun was working with the brilliant, magnificently creative Steve Ditko. He was, and still is, one of the few artists in the biz who has a style so unique you can recognize it anywhere. When I saw the first few sketches he made of Spider-Man I knew he was the perfect illustrator for the series. Thanks to Steve, Spidey never looked like any other hero. He was as unique and distinctive as any comic book character could possibly be. When Steve drew him as Peter Parker, he was just an ordinary, average-looking kid. But when the dazzlin' Mr. D put him in costume, everything about our wondrous web-slinger looked spidery, from the way he curved his fingers to the way his body moved, and who could forget the twisting and angling of his arms and legs? I used to suspect that ol' Steve undoubtedly kept a trained spider around to use for reference, but never could prove it!"[1]

Stan wrote using the "Marvel Method", where the writer would give a plot outline to the artist, the artist would then draw the pages and the writer would write dialogue to go with the art. As with any creative partnership, Steve and Stan sometimes had very different creative philosophies and part of the power of Spider-Man comes from this duality. It's too easy to cast Steve as the reclusive Peter Parker and Stan as the wisecracking Spider-Man – there are elements of both men in each part of Spider-Man, and when these elements came together, they became bottled lightning.

--- **KEY TO PLATE** ---

1: Amazing Adult Fantasy #12
Before Spider-Man, the comic was called Amazing Adult Fantasy, not Amazing Fantasy.

2: AAF #12
Stan Lee and Steve Ditko had worked together for years before they created Spider-Man.

3: Amazing Spider-Man Annual #1
Stan and Steve enjoyed poking fun at their working relationship.

ALONG CAME A SPIDER

No one expected Spider-Man to be a hit, let alone the most popular super hero in the world. In 1962, Stan Lee had just launched the *Fantastic Four* comic to great commercial success and was searching for something new. Looking at the newsstands, Stan saw that something was missing from super hero comics – a character that his teenage readers could identify with. Super heroes were almost all adults, with teenagers being relegated to the sidekick or supporting character role.

A science fiction anthology comic, *Amazing Adult Fantasy* was about to close, and so for its final issue (where it would be renamed *Amazing Fantasy*), Stan persuaded publisher Martin Goodman to let him try out a new hero called Spider-Man. After all, this was the last issue – what did Martin have to lose? The idea of Spider-Man was not a popular one, and Stan had to fight to get the comic made. Looking back, he wrote, "It's hard to remember all the arguments that were used to convince me not to feature our friendly neighbourhood wall-crawler in his own series. But, just to give you an idea, here are some of them… You can't name a hero 'Spider-Man' because people hate spiders! You can't feature a teenager as a super hero. Teenagers can only be sidekicks. You can't give a hero so many problems. Readers won't think he's heroic enough. You can't have a hero who isn't big and glamorous and handsome."[2]

Determined to prove the naysayers wrong, Stan initially approached veteran Marvel artist Jack Kirby, who had recently had success with *Fantastic Four*. Jack's initial idea was for the story to be about a boy who had a magic ring that gave him super powers. He drew the first six pages but Stan found that they were too bold and heroic – they didn't capture teenage life in quite the right way. He needed someone who could create something different from all the other super hero comics, so he turned to Steve Ditko.

Steve drew the interior pages for this new version, while Jack provided a dynamic cover for the retitled *Amazing Fantasy #15*, with this exciting, mysterious character swinging through an urban landscape, clutching a clearly terrified man. Was this masked figure a hero or a villain? Why wasn't he showing his face? Readers would have to buy the comic to find out. Steve's masterful, expressive artwork of Peter Parker showed the teenage angst and anxiety that wasn't seen in comics at the time, but was instantly relatable to his audience. His Spider-Man was a wiry, brooding figure, quite unlike any other super hero at the time.

Sales of *Amazing Fantasy #15* surpassed all expectations, rapidly becoming one of Marvel's most successful comics. Marvel had another hit on its hands, but no one could predict quite how popular Spider-Man would become. As Stan explained, "The [...] wall-crawler, who violated every rule in comic-book-publishing history, became the most popular super hero in all of comicbookdom! And the more unique and more offbeat we made him, the more his popularity grew."[3]

───────────────────────── **KEY TO PLATE** ─────────────────────────

1: Amazing Fantasy #15
Steve Ditko's version of the original cover for Spidey's first appearance

gives a very different view of the web-slinger.

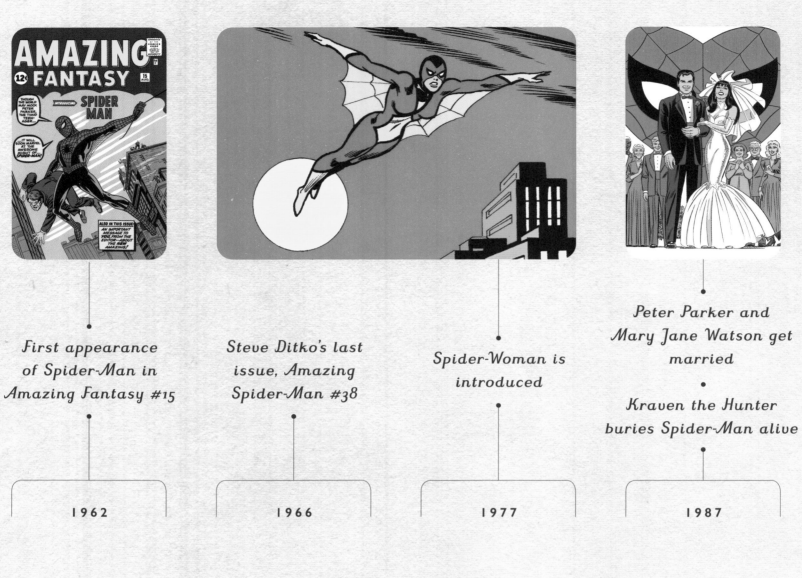

First appearance
of Spider-Man in
Amazing Fantasy #15

Steve Ditko's last
issue, Amazing
Spider-Man #38

Spider-Woman is
introduced

Peter Parker and
Mary Jane Watson get
married

Kraven the Hunter
buries Spider-Man alive

1962	1966	1977	1987

1963	1973	1984	1988

Gets his own comic
in Amazing
Spider-Man #1

Gwen Stacy dies

Spidey gets a new
black costume

Eddie Brock
merges with the
symbiote costume
to become Venom

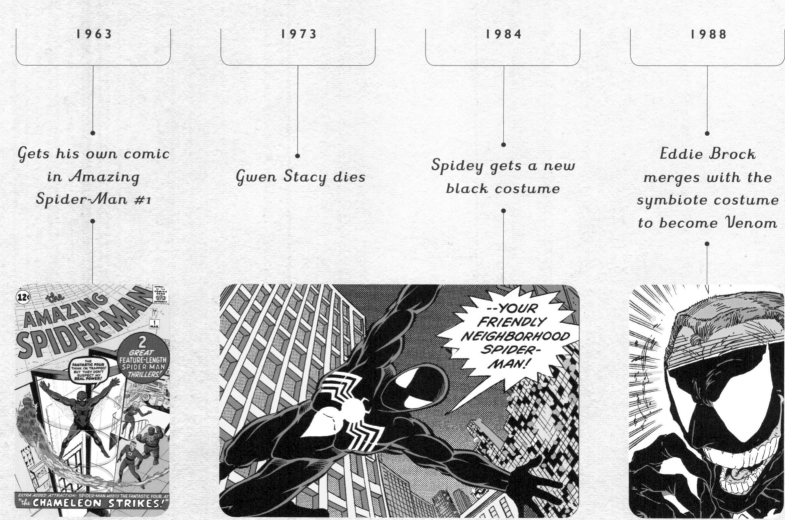

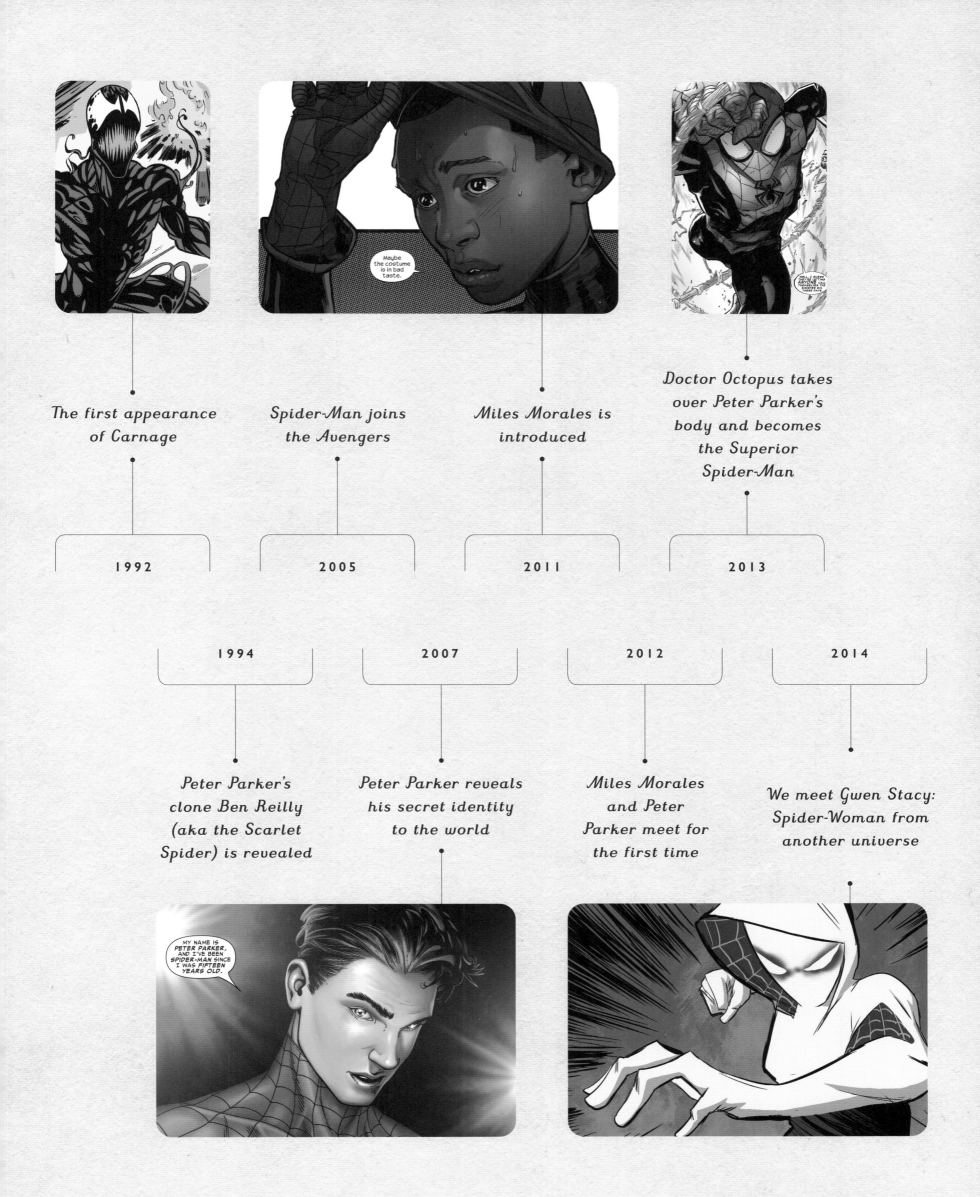

The first appearance
of Carnage

Spider-Man joins
the Avengers

Miles Morales is
introduced

Doctor Octopus takes
over Peter Parker's
body and becomes
the Superior
Spider-Man

1992

2005

2011

2013

1994

2007

2012

2014

Peter Parker's
clone Ben Reilly
(aka the Scarlet
Spider) is revealed

Peter Parker reveals
his secret identity
to the world

Miles Morales
and Peter
Parker meet for
the first time

We meet Gwen Stacy:
Spider-Woman from
another universe

SECTION 2

GREAT POWERS

CREATOR SPOTLIGHT:

JOHN ROMITA SR AND JOHN ROMITA JR

If there's one name that has become synonymous with Spider-Man's art, it's Romita. Starting with *Amazing Spider-Man #38* in 1966, John Romita Sr was responsible for shaping the look of a whole generation of Marvel comics. As Stan Lee put it at the time, "John Romita Sr. is certifiably as talented and legendary as any creative genius who ever left a giant imprint in the hallowed halls of Marvel!"[4] His son, John Romita Jr, started working in comics in 1977, with his first story in *Amazing Spider-Man Annual #11*, and has been an industry-changing force in comics ever since, revolutionising the look of Spider-Man again and again.

Taking over the reins of *Amazing Spider-Man* from Steve Ditko was a daunting prospect, but Romita Sr slowly built in his own art style over the issues, continuing to shape Peter Parker's world. The key to his success was his storytelling, imbuing every story with the drama, pathos and emotion that made Spider-Man a hit. "I told the story the way [Stan] liked it," remembered Romita Sr. "We saw eye to eye on that. Where the stories come first, the characters come first. Not the artwork. [...] My philosophy is that when the artwork gets to be too obvious, and it's done for sensationalism... when it starts to become more important than the story, you're really defeating yourself."[5]

"The characters we rolled out during my years on *Amazing Spider-Man* were my

FIRST SKETCH OF MARY JANE WATSON 1966

①

②

pride and joy," said Romita Sr. "Stan would leave an index card tacked to my board before each plotting meeting with a name on it… no description or powers… just names such as 'Shocker', 'Rhino', 'the Kingpin', 'the Prowler' and others over the years. He let the names evoke their distinct abilities and behaviours."[6]

Romita Jr was always aware of his father's connection to Spider-Man. "Ever since my father told my brother and me that Spider-Man/Peter Parker lived close to our home in Queens, NYC, we were hooked!" he explains. "We talked Spider-Man on long drives to family get-togethers, and it was as if we had an extra family member!"[7]

Romita Jr brought a breath of fresh air to Spider-Man, with his unparalleled skill in composition and pacing. His Spider-Man stories are brilliantly dynamic and visually impactful, giving the wall crawler levels of energy never before seen. Romita Jr remembers the pressure of following such hallowed footsteps. "As luck would also have it, I was able to watch the greatest Spider-Man artist, my father, John, work with the greatest Spider-Man writer, Stan, on the greatest character of all time. Fortunately, after joining the comic book universe, I was given a chance to work on this great character, the Amazing Spider-Man. I was terrified! How do I follow my father? How do I follow any of the previous Spidey artists? I had no idea, but I stuck it out and got lucky."[8]

KEY TO PLATE

1: Sketch of Mary Jane Watson
The first ever sketch of Mary Jane Watson by John Romita Sr.

2: Marvel Age #111
Marvel's magazine celebrates the impact of John Romita Sr.

3: Amazing Spider-Man Annual #5
Artist Marie Severin pokes playful fun at the work practices of Stan Lee, John Romita and Stan's brother Larry Lieber.

4: ASM Annual #5
The creators having a friendly disagreement!

PETER PARKER'S HOME LIFE

Part of the enduring appeal of Spider-Man is the everyman nature of Peter Parker. Readers find it easy to empathise with this regular Joe who just can't seem to catch a break. Stan Lee would shrewdly later comment, "You can practically measure a hero's popularity by the amount of trouble he manages to get himself into."[9] Peter Parker wasn't a millionaire playboy, a strapping super soldier or a Norse God of Thunder, he was a gawky teenager from Queens who was ostracised by his peers. While the Fantastic Four were wrestling with world-devouring monsters from the Negative Zone, Peter was asking girls out for dates and being rejected. Stan knew exactly what he was doing, describing him in his first appearance as "The World's most amazing teenager, Spider-Man, the super hero who could be you!"

A sadness haunts Peter — his story hints at tragedy before it even starts. He lives with his Uncle Ben and Aunt May, not his parents, implying that a catastrophe has taken place before we've even met Peter. His parents, Richard and Mary Parker, would not be discussed until 1968's *Spider-Man Annual #5*. Peter's suburban home in Queens is modest and unassuming, clearly influenced by Steve Ditko's midwestern upbringing. In fact, many of the vistas, scenes and buildings (including Peter's Midtown High School), are referenced from Steve's hometown of Johnstown, Pennsylvania.

The supporting cast of characters were types that would be well known to Spider-Man's teenage audience. The awkward Peter is mocked by jocks, rejected by girls and laughed at by his classmates. Many of Peter's classmates became permanent fixtures within expanding and evolving narratives. Decades later, high school bully Flash Thompson became Spider-Man's ally, Agent Anti-Venom, a super soldier with a symbiotic alien suit. Thwarted love interest Liz Allan married Peter's college friend Harry Osborn and later became CEO of megacorporation Alchemax.

Peter is happiest when he is with his aunt and uncle who dote on him. We are told that his Uncle Ben "thought he was a pretty special lad", while Aunt May "thought the sun rose and set upon her nephew". When disaster strikes and Uncle Ben is killed by a robber, it hits the reader so much harder because we know that this is the only part of Peter's life where he was truly content.

Peter's life after Uncle Ben's death is a complicated web of tangled responsibilities, one that would be very relatable to Spider-Man's audience. Peter is worried about affording medicine for his sickly Aunt May, frets about his schoolwork and shies away from social engagements with his classmates — all of this before he even starts thinking about his super hero secret identity.

KEY TO PLATE

1: Amazing Spider-Man Annual #1
A typical scene in Peter Parker's science class!

2: ASM Annual #1
Pete's house, located on a quiet street in the Forest Hills section of New York, where he lives with his doting Aunt May.

3: The ASM #1
Part of the appeal of Peter Parker is that he could never catch a break.

FRIENDLY NEIGHBOURHOOD SPIDER-MAN

Peter Parker got his powers when he was bitten by a radioactive spider at a science exhibition, which gave him the proportional strength, speed and endurance of a spider. He was also able to devise a formula for his webbing, a thin, glue-like substance that is strong enough to tie up his enemies and allow him to swing through New York, but which also dissolves after an hour. And his Spider-Sense, that warns of danger, allows him to stay one step ahead of his very large roster of villains.

Steve Ditko's design for the Spider-Man costume is brilliant in its simplicity, and it's a testament to his work that the design has barely changed in 60 years. Spider-Man is identifiable from almost any part of his costume because of his bold and striking design, and the fact that the costume covers him completely means that readers can identify with him, as it could be anyone wearing the suit.

Spider-Man's early adventures are characterised by exciting battles with dangerous, experienced villains who contrast with Peter's youth and naivety. Spider-Man's priorities are different from other super heroes. In *Amazing Spider-Man #1* he is primarily concerned with making money to pay for medicine for Aunt May. After finding it impossible to cash a cheque for his TV appearances made out to "Spider-Man", he tries to join the Fantastic Four before finding out that the FF do not pay a salary.

One of the reasons that Spider-Man is so relatable is that we spend so much time in the hero's head. Stan Lee said, "one of the things that has, over the years, set Spidey apart from other super heroes is the fact that he so often agonises over the hand that fate has dealt him [...] The ol' wall-crawler is considered by many to be the Hamlet of super-herodom. In fact, people always ask what made me decide to give Spider-Man so many thought balloons, as we all call them in comic-book land, because it seems nobody ever used thought balloons quite that way until Aunt May's neurotic nephew made the scene. Well, the reason is quite simple, really. In novels, a reader is usually privy to the protagonist's thoughts. That's what helps make characters come alive in our imagination; it makes us feel we know them. Likewise, in stage plays, and in comics as well, we can gain great insights into the characters by their conversation. But Spidey, alas, is a loner. When he's out wall-crawling or web-slinging [...] he's all by himself. He has no one to talk to at such times."[10]

KEY TO PLATE

1: The Amazing Spider-Man #4
Peter Parker realises that with great power comes great responsibility.

2: The ASM #1
Spider-Man soon got his own comic, which guest-starred the Fantastic Four in the first issue.

3: The Amazing Spider-Man Annual #1
Steve Ditko exhibits his iconic style in all its glory, showing off Spidey's impressive abilities.

SPIDER-MAN'S RELATIONSHIPS

One of the first things that we learn about Peter Parker is his unrequited longing for romantic companionship. Within five panels of meeting Parker in *Amazing Fantasy #15* we see him asking out Sally Avril, who brusquely rejects him with "You're just not my type… not when dream boats like Flash Thompson are around!", setting the scene for the hero's troubled love life.

As the comic progressed, more characters and potential love interests were introduced; his love life was never easy. When Peter started working as a freelance photographer at the *Daily Bugle*, he struck up a friendship with J. Jonah Jameson's long-suffering assistant Betty Brant. The two had a natural rapport, and she caught a glimpse of the tortured inner life that Peter tried hard to hide. Betty became Peter's first girlfriend, but she was always suspicious of how he disappeared at the first sign of trouble, and she eventually ended the relationship when she suspected he had feelings for his classmate Liz Allan.

Tragedy has always swirled around the foundations of Spider-Man's story. Peter's relationship with Gwen Stacy was one that would change him forever. Gwen was a fellow student at Empire State University who shared Peter's love of science. Peter and Gwen dated for years until in *Amazing Spider-Man #121* Gwen died during a battle between Spider-Man and the Green Goblin. Gwen's death represents a turning point in Spider-Man's story and is one that was very carefully considered. Writer Gerry Conway and editor Roy Thomas wanted to provide a death that was meaningful and would have an impact on readers.

Peter did not just date as Peter Parker, but also as Spider-Man. In the course of his super hero career, Spider-Man has dated Captain Marvel, Kitty Pryde, Mockingbird, Silk and Silver Sable but his longest relationship was with Felicia Hardy, the Black Cat. The relationship between Spider-Man and the jewel thief Black Cat started flirtatiously, and the two became romantically involved. While dating Spider-Man, Black Cat had little time for Peter and at times demanded that he put his mask back on when he removed it.

The recurring love of Peter's life has always been Mary Jane Watson. Introduced as a running gag, Peter spent many issues trying to avoid a blind date set up by Aunt May, and of course when Peter finally does meet her, she is a knockout. "Face it Tiger, you just hit the jackpot!" grins Mary Jane, in one of the most iconic panels in the comic's history. Modern, fashionable and dynamic, Mary Jane was a breath of fresh air, and was hugely popular with fans. Peter and MJ married in *Amazing Spider-Man Annual #21* in 1987, while Stan Lee officiated a real event in Shea Stadium with actors portraying the happy couple.

Sadly, Peter and MJ would not remain married forever…

──────────────── **KEY TO PLATE** ────────────────

1: **The Amazing Spider-Man #122**
The aftermath of Gwen's death spells fatal danger for the Green Goblin.

2: **The ASM #194**
Spider-Man's worthy enemy Black Cat, and sometimes girlfriend, makes her smashing debut.

3: **Amazing Spider-Man Annual #21**
Peter Parker dreams of Spidey's wedding, with a gallery of villains in attendance!

THE DAILY BUGLE

Spider-Man is perhaps the only super hero who is employed by an organisation that is actively trying to destroy his reputation. J. Jonah Jameson, originally depicted by Steve Ditko as a leering hyena of a human being, is first seen in *Amazing Spider-Man #1*, a newspaper publisher desperate to prove that Spider-Man is a menace, regardless of the facts. Jonah is humanised by his love for his son, the courageous test pilot John Jameson. When John Jameson's rocket launch goes wrong, he is saved by Spider-Man, but Jonah's response, as ever, is "This newspaper demands that Spider-Man be arrested and prosecuted!"

Jonah grows to become a complex and interesting character, sometimes bombastic, sometimes remorseful. Writers who took over after Stan would often base Jonah's speech patterns on Stan himself. Jonah, the publisher of the *Daily Bugle*, is almost always depicted as being loyal to his staff and friends, and living by his own code of conduct. As Stan would later write, "Make no mistake about it. Jolly Jonah is not a villain. He's not a bad guy. He just marches to the beat of a different drummer. Just like Captain Queeg in *The Caine Mutiny*, Jonah and his ilk are part of the fabric of America. We may not want to party with them, but life would surely be a whole lot duller if they weren't around."[11]

As compelling a character as Jonah is, he needed characters to bounce off of at the *Daily Bugle*, and so he was soon joined by long-suffering secretary Betty Brant in *Amazing Spider-Man #4* and then editor-in-chief Robbie Robertson was introduced in *Amazing Spider-Man #51*. Both characters tend to act as foils to Jonah, with Robbie often sticking up for Spider-Man when Jonah treats him unfairly. As one of the first African American characters to play a supporting role in super hero comics, Robertson became a popular addition to the comic, and his backstory was fleshed out in a 1988 storyline in *Peter Parker: Spectacular Spider-Man*. It was revealed that Robertson had grown up in Harlem with Spider-Man villain Tombstone where he had been intimidated into not reporting his crimes.

Part of the joy of the *Daily Bugle* is that it feels like a modern, alive workplace. *The Bugle*'s newsroom has bustled with supporting characters over the years. Investigative reporter Ned Leeds married Betty Brant and briefly became the Hobgoblin, while fellow reporter and Daredevil supporting character Ben Urich has often worked with photographer Peter Parker.

The *Daily Bugle* itself has also changed over the years; at first readers only caught brief glimpses of Jonah's desk, but soon readers saw a bustling, forty-six storey building with the newspaper's logo in 30-foot letters on the roof. One of the staples of Jonah's office was an open window for Spider-Man (or villains) to climb through, with Spidey using this as a way of webbing Jonah's trousers to his chair in *Amazing Spider-Man #4*. Like any newspaper, the *Daily Bugle* has been forced to change with the times; it was bought out by rival publisher Dexter Bennet and rebranded as *The DB!* before the original staff brought the *Daily Bugle* name back.

KEY TO PLATE

1: Amazing Spider-Man Annual #5
A typical day at the *Daily Bugle*.

2: Daily Bugle #2
The *Daily Bugle* is a rich source for stories in Spider-Man's world.

3: The Amazing Spider-Man #9
J. Jonah Jameson has his own code of conduct, which does not preclude him from underpaying Peter Parker.

SECTION 3

GREAT RESPONSIBILITIES

CREATOR SPOTLIGHT:

TODD MCFARLANE AND DAVID MICHELINIE

One of the exciting and compelling things about Spider-Man is seeing how his cast of villains and allies has grown as the character developed. David Michelinie wrote *Amazing Spider-Man* from 1987 to 1994, introducing characters such as Venom and Carnage, who instantly became hits. "Venom became very popular," recalled David. "He appealed to me particularly because he was created for only one purpose: to kill Spider-Man. At the time there weren't any other villains who actually wanted to kill Spidey. Most of Spider-Man's rogues' gallery just wanted to avoid him. I liked the purity of Venom's motivation."[12]

The secret of David's take on Spider-Man comes from a genuine admiration for the character. "I've always liked dealing with the person," said David. "Peter Parker with the suit is still Peter Parker… He is a real person with problems. He has a noble sensibility and a solid moral code. No matter what complications are thrown his way, he always retains his values."[13]

In 1988 David was joined by artist Todd McFarlane, which provided a once in a generation buzz around the character. The combination of electrifying writing coupled with a dynamic new visual take on Spidey was quickly snapped up by fans. Superstar artist Todd wowed readers with his updated but classic look on Spider-Man. "I didn't go back to the same look [readers] were used to," explained Todd. "I threw in the big eyes and the different webbing and everything else. It was a new look for the old look. My intention was that even if you posed the character in silhouette, so you couldn't see the costume, you would still know that it was Spider-Man."[14]

The brilliant and bombastic art style of Todd was grounded by the exciting but relatable stories of David. "It's [easy] to identify with a guy who has to struggle to cope with his powers and the same everyday problems that you or I have," said David. "If we'd been bitten by a radioactive spider would we have become Spider-Man? Probably not. Peter Parker is a very special character, and I'm glad I got the chance to write about him. *Amazing Spider-Man* was my dream job."[15] In 1990 Todd launched a new Spider-Man comic, taking on both the art and writing of the comic. The adjective-less *Spider-Man #1* was a phenomenon, selling millions of copies.

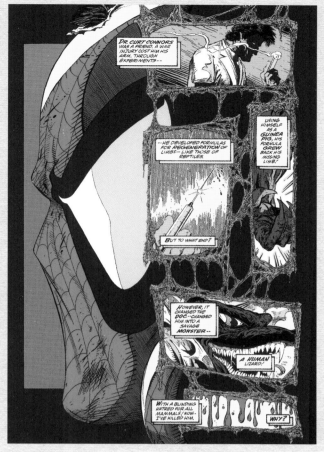

1: Spider-Man #1

The dynamic new iteration of Spider-Man by artist Todd McFarlane.

2: SM #2

Todd's style perfectly complemented David Michelinie's darker and more dynamic Spidey.

4: ASM #300

Todd McFarlane gave Spider-Man dense, intricate webs to travel around New York.

3: Amazing Spider-Man #300

The 25th anniversary special showcased Spidey in his black suit.

THE SINISTER SIX

As Spider-Man's adventures grew, so did his rogues' gallery. Part of Stan Lee's genius was creating an interconnected universe, where characters could move fluidly from one story to another. If heroes could team up, like they had done in 1963's *Avengers #1*, then why couldn't villains do the same thing? "Back then, in the 60s, we were so thrilled and grateful for the wonderful reception Spidey was given by the reading public that we wanted to return the favour," explained Stan about the decision to bring the villains together in *Amazing Spider-Man Annual #1*. "The best thing we could think of doing for our [...] public was to produce a 41-page super-spectacular of ol' Web-Head featuring six, count 'em, six of our maddest, baddest, most stultifyin' super-villains in one fabulous, far-out, fast-moving yarn!"[16]

The Vulture, Doctor Octopus, the Sandman, Electro, Mysterio and Kraven the Hunter were introduced in *Amazing Spider-Man* issues 2, 3, 4, 9, 13 and 15 respectively, but in 1964's *Amazing Spider-Man Annual #1* they joined forces for the first time to become the Sinister Six, in what was billed on the cover as "Spidey's longest, greatest battle". Assembled by Doctor Octopus, the plan was simply to wear Spider-Man down one by one – it wasn't until the *Return of the Sinister Six* storyline in *Amazing Spider-Man #334* that they would attack en masse.

One of the many reasons for the enduring appeal of Spider-Man is his deep and wide-ranging rogues' gallery. Not only does Peter Parker feel the intense pressures of a teenager, but he's also often seemingly outclassed – a scrappy underdog fighting enemies who appear to be more than a match for him. The Sinister Six represent Spider-Man's refusal to give up, even against overwhelming odds. Almost all of Spider-Man's early villains are older than him – after the death of his Uncle Ben, most of the adults in Spider-Man's life were trying to destroy him. Many villains, like Peter, are the results of science experiments gone wrong – cautionary reflections of what he could have been.

Over the years, the roster of the Sinister Six has changed, subbing in new villains for deceased, inactive, reformed or recalcitrant members. The sheer number of Spider-Man villains means that different groups have, at times, been forced to call themselves the Sinister Seven, Sinister Twelve, Sinister Sixteen and even the Sinister Sixty Six.

KEY TO PLATE

1: Amazing Spider-Man Annual #1
The first team-up of Spider-Man's greatest enemies, the Sinister Six.

2: Amazing Spider-Man #334
Years later Doctor Octopus re-formed the Sinister Six.

3: ASM #338
The line-up of the team has changed over the years, bringing in new members like Hobgoblin to replace dead or missing members like Kraven.

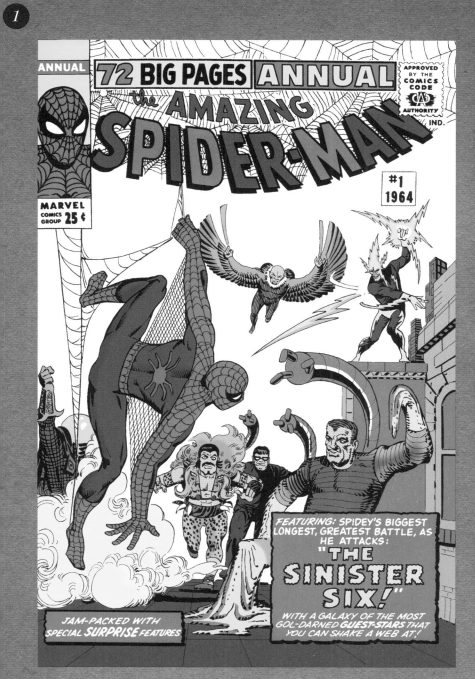

SPIDER-MAN NO MORE!

A huge part of the story of Spider-Man is the push and pull between Peter Parker and his super hero alter ego. Peter's life would be so much easier without the burden of Spider-Man, and he is constantly reminded of that fact.

1967's *Amazing Spider-Man #50* shows Peter completely rejecting Spider-Man. In a story titled *Spider-Man No More!* he is pushed to his limits — his life as Spider-Man meant that he had no time for study, romance or friendship and, worst of all, is late to help Aunt May when she is dangerously ill. It's an anti-Spider-Man polemic from J. Jonah Jameson that pushed him over the edge. Peter threw the Spider-Man suit in the rubbish and walked away, thinking to himself, "I was just a young, unthinking teenager when I first became Spider-Man [...] and every boy… sooner or later… must put away his toys… and become… a man!"

Stan Lee was keen to highlight the psychological nature of the story. "Beginning with the cover, which I feel is one of the most effective we've ever done [...], this story probes into Spidey's psyche more deeply than any written before. It deals with our hero being faced with so many personal problems, caused by his Spider-Man identity, that he finally figures he'd have to be nuts to remain a super hero, considering all the grief it has brought him [...] And that's when the unexpected drama really starts. I remember when the story first appeared we were besieged by letters from psychology students telling us that *Spider-Man No More* was the chief topic of discussion in their classes for days!"[17]

By the end of the issue, Peter was back in the Spider-Man costume, realising that his responsibility to help others is too great. Fifty issues later, however, in *Amazing Spider-Man #100*, Parker still struggled with this exact same problem. "Maybe I'm finally growing up, at last," Spider-Man said to himself. "Maybe I'm starting to realise there's more to life than being a corny costumed clown." Peter wanted a normal life with Gwen Stacy without the spectre of Spider-Man haunting him, so he created a serum to remove his powers. Sadly, this potion didn't work and resulted in Spider-Man gaining four extra arms for the rest of the issue. While this was soon rectified, Peter's lingering resentment of Spider-Man remained.

There are other moments, too, when Peter has given up his Spider-Man identity. Once, when Peter's clone Ben Reilly took on the role of Spider-Man and again when Spider-Man had a bounty placed on his head, forcing Peter to take on four other identities to confuse the police. One thing has always remained constant, Uncle Ben's motto that with great power there must also come great responsibility.

──────────── **KEY TO PLATE** ────────────

1: Amazing Spider-Man #50
Frustrated with his life, Peter Parker decides to throw away his Spider-Man outfit.

2: ASM #100
Peter ponders life again without his super hero identity.

3: ASM #100
Peter creates a potion that he hopes will rid him of his powers. Upon drinking the potion, he finds that he's grown four extra arms!

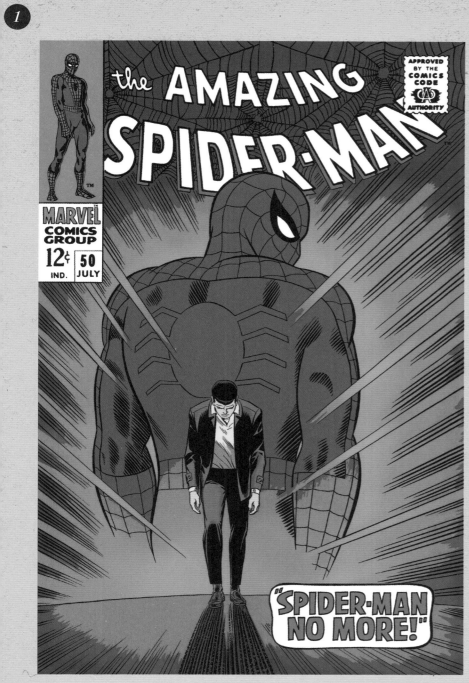

THE NIGHT GWEN STACY DIED

Perhaps the most shocking event in Spider-Man's history is the death of his girlfriend Gwen Stacy. Deaths in comic books at the time were often reversible, with characters sometimes returning in the same issue. This was something different.

Writer Gerry Conway explained the reason for such a dramatic storyline. "John Romita felt – we all felt, Stan Lee and Roy Thomas (then editor-in-chief) and yours truly – that Spider-Man's life had become too placid, too safe, too... normal. Despite some terrific individual stories over the previous few years (the drug issue, Captain Stacy's death, the introduction of the Kingpin) we had a sense that Peter's life had settled into a, well, rut. He faced villains; he was misunderstood by society; he had minor problems but come right down to it, things were going pretty well for our friendly neighbourhood web-slinger. It was time to shake things up. John believed somebody had to die, to remind the reader (and Peter) that the world was a harsh place, heroes couldn't save everyone, and sometimes death could not be escaped."[18]

The tragic events of *Amazing Spider-Man #121* came at the culmination of a long-running story arc. Maniacal supervillain the Green Goblin had long been revealed to be Norman Osborn, the father of Peter Parker's best friend, Harry Osborn. Like most father-figures in Spider-Man's world, Norman is up to no good; although he is a

successful and wealthy industrialist, he leaves a legacy of violence and anger for his son, Harry and Harry buckles under the pressure, becoming addicted to drugs.

Norman is aware of Peter's secret identity, and he blames him for Harry's condition. As the Green Goblin, he kidnaps Gwen and throws her from the Brooklyn Bridge. Spider-Man rushes to save her, but he is too late and by the time he has fired a web to catch her she has fallen too far to be saved. The story left Gwen's fate in no doubt, her neck had snapped from the force of the fall. Norman is killed, but it is of little consolation to the bereft Peter.

The death of Gwen was shocking to fans who had seen Peter's relationship with her grow, and this moment of tragedy informs every Spider-Man story going forward. The fact that Peter was unable to save his own girlfriend shows the terrible strains of his great responsibility. As Conway put it, "Peter's grief and anger over the death of Gwen Stacy is more intense and pervasive than anything we experienced in comics before 1973. It lasts longer, goes deeper, and has greater repercussions than any previous emotional response. And it expands outward to affect everyone around him. It transforms Peter's relationship with Mary Jane, Harry Osborn, even J. Jonah Jameson. Peter's grief is a wound, like true emotional wounds in real life, that never fully heals."[19]

KEY TO PLATE

1: The Amazing Spider-Man #121
One of Spider-Man's most iconic covers warns of the death of a key cast member.

2: The ASM #121
The Green Goblin was always one of Spider-Man's most dangerous villains.

3: The ASM #121
The fatal moment in Spider-Man's life that would alter comic book history.

4: The ASM #121
Spider-Man comes to terms with Gwen Stacy's death and swears revenge.

FRIENDLY SYMBIOTE VENOM MAN!

By 1984, Spider-Man had been in the same costume for over 20 years. He needed a new look, but how do you update something as timeless as Steve Ditko's original design? Artist Ron Frenz showcased the bold new costume with a cover that riffed on Jack Kirby's classic *Amazing Fantasy #15*, demonstrating the difference in look and tone. "Never before had a super hero as well known and successful as Spidey changed his appearance," explains *Amazing Spider-Man* editor Jim Salicrup. "Changing Spidey's costume was tampering with success, something only the batty Bullpen would be crazy enough to dare!"[20]

The reason for the change was that Spidey had ripped his old costume on Battleworld as part of the *Secret Wars* event. Spider-Man finds a machine that he thinks is going to give him a new costume, but we soon find out that the costume is actually an alien symbiote, joined to Spidey on a psychic level. The new costume proved so popular with readers that, even when Spider-Man was separated from the alien, he kept the look, sporting a copy of the costume created by Black Cat.

One important aspect of Spider-Man's costume didn't change – the fact that it still covered his whole body. It was important to keep the idea that Spider-Man could be anybody under the outfit. While the trademark webbing was gone, the distinctive spider symbol would identify Spider-Man from other heroes.

The black costume literally took on a life of its own after separating from Spider-Man. It bonded with Peter Parker's work rival, Eddie Brock, to become Venom – who instantly became one of Spider-Man's greatest enemies. A distorted reflection of Spider-Man, Venom is a complicated antihero who embraced his role as a "lethal protector". Venom was an instant hit with fans and his popularity grew because he wasn't overused at first – he hovered in the shadows of other Spider-Man stories.

Serial killer Cletus Cassidy bonded with an offspring of Venom's symbiote to produce Carnage, a creature stronger than Venom or Spider-Man. Carnage was introduced in 1992 by writer David Michelinie, as a way of highlighting Venom's moral code. Venom's twisted morality of only attacking the guilty contrasts sharply with the sadistic amorality of Carnage.

As Venom's popularity spread, so did the backstory of the alien symbiote costume, building up to the 2021 *King in Black* event, where Knull, the king and creator of the symbiotes, attacks Earth with a symbiote army.

KEY TO PLATE

1: Amazing Spider-Man #252
Ron Frenz referenced *Amazing Fantasy #15* to showcase the new costume.

2: Secret Wars #8
Spider-Man's costume was given to

him on an alien planet.

3: Peter Parker: The Spectacular Spider-Man #101
The new costume allowed artists to create bold, exciting visuals.

4: Venom: Lethal Protector #1
The symbiote costume joined with Eddie Brock to form...Venom!

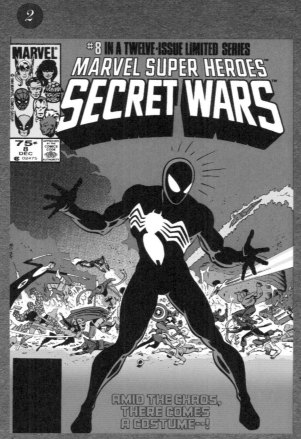

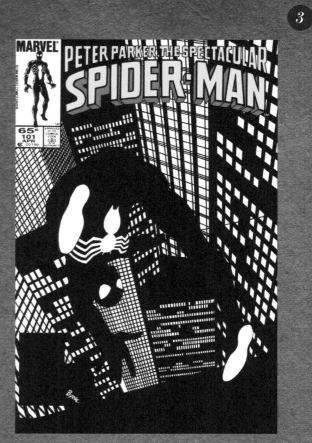

KRAVEN'S LAST HUNT

First introduced in *Amazing Spider-Man #15*, Kraven the Hunter was a core Spider-Man villain. A founding member of the Sinister Six, Kraven (real name Sergei Kravinoff) was a Russian immigrant who had fashioned himself to be the greatest big-game hunter in the world, and what bigger game was there than Spider-Man?

In 1987, writer J. M. DeMatteis took the character in a new direction, showing him as a soulful and tortured Russian aristocrat, driven by a compulsion he could not fully articulate to prove his worth to a family long dead. "I like to hook into a character and keep pushing," explained DeMatteis. "Here we have a villain who's been around for 25 years. Who is he? How did he get that way? I like to write stories where the reader finds himself showing concern not only for the hero, but also for the villain and everyone else."[21]

Running in the *Amazing Spider-Man*, *Peter Parker: the Spectacular Spider-Man* and *Web of Spider-Man* comics at the same time, this was a pivotal moment in Spider-Man comics. *Kraven's Last Hunt* is perhaps best seen in the context of darker, more complex storylines of Marvel at the time, such as *Daredevil: Born Again*, *X-Men: Days of Future Past* and *The Death of Captain Marvel*.

In the story, Kraven, haunted to the point of delirium by his own past failures, finally defeated Spider-Man and buried him alive. Kraven then took Spider-Man's identity, patrolling the city in a copy of Spider-Man's black costume in an effort to prove that he was superior to Spider-Man. Spider-Man dug his way out of his own grave and discovered that he had been buried for two weeks, due to the heavy effects of Kraven's tranquiliser darts. When Spider-Man confronted him, Kraven releases Vermin, a villain who Kraven was able to defeat but Spider-Man was not. When Spider-Man was once again unable to defeat Vermin, it gives Kraven a sense of peace.

Fearful Symmetry: Kraven's Last Hunt is one of the most nuanced, complex and literary Spider-Man stories, taking its full name from William Blake's poem 'The Tyger', while brilliantly weaving together ideas of identity, duty and heroism. DeMatteis places Kraven in the Russian literary tradition, casting him as a doomed, noble hero battling his own internal demons while simultaneously fighting external enemies. In a way, all Spider-Man stories are about responsibility, but in this story we see how someone can twist and warp the ideas that make Spider-Man who he is.

KEY TO PLATE

1: Amazing Spider-Man #294
Kraven finally proves his superiority over Spider-Man.

2: Web of Spider-Man #32

In epic fashion, Spider-Man emerges from his grave.

3: WOSP #32
Spidey escapes and stumbles upon

Kraven's mansion.

4: WOSP #32
Spider-Man confronts his impersonator.

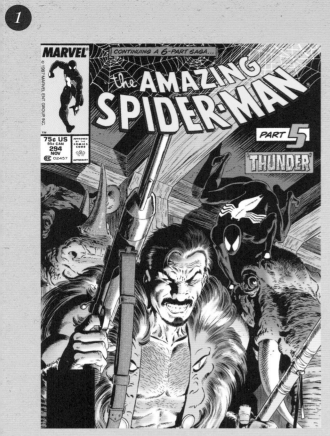

THE CLONE SAGA

Spider-Man's foe the Jackal was secretly Peter Parker and Gwen Stacy's biology professor Miles Warren. During a 1975 storyline, Miles Warren, driven mad by the death of Gwen Stacy, created clones of both Peter and Gwen, and in doing so discovered Spider-Man's secret identity. Spider-Man and his clone fought, and the clone seemingly died.

Years later it was revealed that the clone of Peter hadn't died, but instead had escaped and started a new life under the name Ben Reilly (taken from Peter's Uncle Ben and Aunt May's maiden name). Years later Ben Reilly returned, using the super hero identity of the Scarlet Spider. Ben Reilly and Peter teamed up to fight the Jackal and Kaine, an imperfect clone of Spider-Man. After a climactic battle, Ben Reilly and Peter discovered that Ben Reilly was the original Spider-Man and Peter had been the clone all along. Peter decided to retire from being a super hero to concentrate on his marriage to Mary Jane, passing the role of Spider-Man to Ben Reilly. There was a new Spider-Man in town – Ben Reilly!

The Clone Saga was the biggest thing to happen to Spider-Man in years – an ambitious and far-reaching event that drew on years of continuity and spanned hundreds of comics. Rewriting Spider-Man's history was one thing, but weaving it in with decades-old stories required skill and precision. The sensational nature of *The Clone Saga* meant that the action hopped from Spider-Man book to Spider-Man book, encompassing everything Spider-related that Marvel had published for two years. At one point all titles were briefly renamed "Scarlet Spider" instead of "Spider-Man" to herald the arrival of the new web-slinger. Ben Reilly was later proved to be the clone and Peter the original, and this was all part of a nefarious plot by the recently resurrected Green Goblin.

The different clones of Peter Parker had been firmly established as part of Spider-Man lore. Ben Reilly and Kaine – the first, imperfect clone – would reappear in Peter's life again and again, showing him different versions of how his life could have been.

KEY TO PLATE

1: Amazing Spider-Man #149
The Jackal created an identical clone of Spider-Man.

2: Web of Spider-Man #117
Peter Parker thought that his clone was dead, until he returned years later.

4: WOSP #117
Peter confronts his doppelganger!

3: Web of Scarlet Spider #1
Ben Reilly (AKA the Scarlet Spider) briefly took over Spider-Man comics.

SPIDER-MAN MUSEUM

SECTION 4

BIG TIME

CREATOR SPOTLIGHT:
DAN SLOTT

"Since I was eight years old, writing Spider-Man has been my dream job," admitted Dan Slott.[22] One of the longest-running writers on Spider-Man comics, Dan scripted Spidey stories from 2008 to 2018, shepherding the wall-crawler through some of the biggest events in his history. Dan guided Peter Parker through fame, ruin, heartbreak and death. There is no writer who has taken Spider-Man on quite such a far-reaching journey as Dan has.

Part of the reason for Dan's longevity writing stories for the character is that he realises the range and depth of Spider-Man. "You can't just stick Spidey in a box and say he is a dark urban vigilante who swings through the night to fight crime. Or he's a jokey super hero," explained Dan. "There's all these different things that make up Spider-Man and all these different ways you can tell a Spider-Man story. You see Mike Deodato draw Spider-Man and that's a specific kind of Spider-Man and Humberto Ramos draws him and that's a different kind of Spider-Man. There's something fun about that."[23]

Dan's run on Spider-Man is characterised by bold and brilliant ideas executed in a way that made his titles the "must-have" comics. He has written nine of the top 100 bestselling comics of the 2010s and continues to create a buzz around every comic he touches.

One of the things that Dan didn't expect about writing Spider-Man is how much Spidey would take over his day-to-day life. "There are days where everything gets seen through the Spider-Man filter first," he explained. "If I'm walking down the streets in New York and I notice something, I'd go, 'Oh, how would Spider-Man deal with that?' It's a reflex muscle in the back of your head. Or you read a news story. Something happens and you go, 'What if that was Mysterio?' When you do this for ten years, that's just the way you're wired."[24]

─────────────── **KEY TO PLATE** ───────────────

1: Amazing Spider-Man #560
'Brand New Day' ushered in a new era for Spider-Man.

2: ASM #669
'The Slott Variant' showed Dan saving Spider-Man instead!

3: ASM #568
Spider-Man has always had one of the biggest supporting casts in comics.

THAT MEANS WHEN PUSH COMES TO SHOVE, MY LIFE AS PETER *ALWAYS* HAS TO TAKE A BACKSEAT...

...TO MY SPIDER-SIDE. AND WITH ALL OF THE BAD GUYS I'VE PICKED UP OVER THE YEARS...

THE NEW AVENGERS

Spider-Man and the Avengers have had many adventures together, first teaming up in 1964's *Avengers #11* when Kang attacked the team with a Spider-Man android. Though the Avengers had asked him to join their ranks (in *Amazing Spider-Man Annual #3* and *Avengers* Vol 3 #1) Spider-Man declined. While he occasionally helped the team on a provisional basis, for years Spidey was never a full member of the team.

That was until 2004's *New Avengers #1*. During a massive breakout at the supervillain prison The Raft, Spider-Man becomes part of a team of first responder super heroes along with Iron Man, Captain America, Spider-Woman, Luke Cage and the Sentry. The Avengers had recently disbanded, and Cap took this as a sign that this new team should carry on the Avengers legacy. The idea to add Spider-Man to the Avengers came from a Marvel publishing retreat where creative teams came together to pitch new ideas. Writer Brian Michael Bendis had a simple pitch for the Avengers — it should be a team made up of the coolest heroes that Marvel had to offer. And who was cooler than Spider-Man? Fans agreed and sales of the book rocketed.

Joining the Avengers changed nearly every aspect of Peter Parker's life. Peter and Mary Jane Watson moved into Avengers Tower in Manhattan, Tony Stark's $600 million skyscraper. Peter and Tony became closer, and Iron Man built a new suit of armour for Spider-Man, the Iron Spider suit. Obviously influenced by Iron Man's colour scheme and love of technology, the suit combined cutting-edge nanotechnology with the toughest composite alloys. The most innovative part of the Iron Spider armour is the three spider arms that are stowed in the back of the suit, ready for deployment at any time. Not only are the arms formidable weapons, but they also contain sensors, cameras and scientific equipment.

Although most things changed for Spider-Man, there was one thing that remained the same: J. Jonah Jameson. Despite the fact that the Avengers and the world at large had accepted Spider-Man as a hero, Jonah continued his vendetta against the web-slinger. Keen to stop the bad press about Spidey, Iron Man and Captain America made a deal with Jonah to give the *Daily Bugle* exclusive access to the Avengers in return for the paper toning down the coverage of Spidey. Jonah responds by savaging the rest of the team in the press, saying they are "posed to bury the good name of the Avengers once and for all".

KEY TO PLATE

*1: **New Avengers #59***
Making Spider-Man an Avenger was a bold choice.

*2: **NA #1***
A new team of Avengers for a new era.

*3: **The Avengers #11***
The mighty Avengers meet Spider-Man for the first time.

*4: **The Amazing Spider-Man #529***
Spidey is gifted a new costume from Tony Stark.

*5: **NA #15***
Being an Avenger does have some advantages.

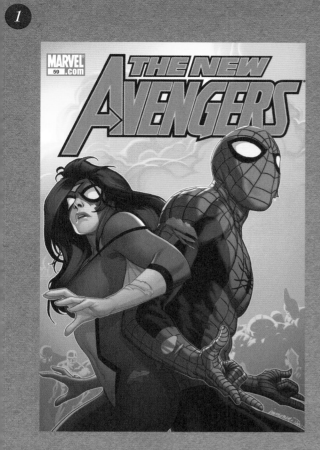

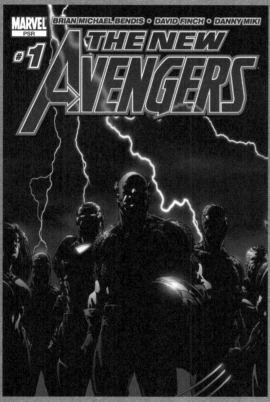

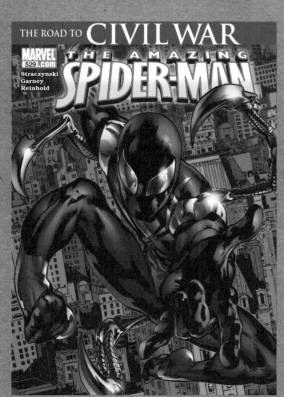

CIVIL WAR

One of the most important things about Spider-Man is his secret identity. Forged in the creation of the character is the death of his Uncle Ben, and the overriding fear that other people he loves could be hurt because of his double life. *Civil War* saw Peter Parker trapped in a schism between Iron Man and Captain America. After a superpower-related tragedy, Tony Stark pushed for the Superhuman Registration Act, which required all super heroes to act under official government regulation, and, most importantly for Spider-Man, register their powers and secret identities. Steve Rogers led a team of super heroes opposed to the act, and this team was quickly forced to go underground.

At first Peter sided with Iron Man, and, in a huge public announcement, unmasked during a press conference supporting the act. Now the whole world knew that Peter was Spider-Man. With true Parker luck, Spider-Man managed to end up in the worst of all possible situations. After revealing his secret identity, Peter fell out with Iron Man over the latter's use of strongarm tactics to enforce the Superhuman Registration Act. Spider-Man joined Captain America's team of renegade objectors and was forced to go on the run with Mary Jane Watson and Aunt May.

Then disaster struck. Aunt May was shot by a bullet meant for Peter and was slowly dying. Peter desperately raced to find a way to save her until he was left with only one option – a literal deal with the devil. The demon Mephisto had been part of Marvel comics since 1968, a Faustian fiend with a penchant for making deals. In return for the restoration of Aunt May's health, Mephisto did not ask for Peter's soul, but instead asked him to sacrifice his marriage to Mary Jane.

Peter and Mary Jane agreed to this bargain, and Peter soon woke up in a new world where he never revealed his secret identity and Aunt May is safe, but he is no longer married to Mary Jane. Mephisto allowed Peter to briefly meet the daughter that he and Mary Jane could have had, before abruptly taking her away. Nothing like this had ever been attempted in Spider-Man before, unpicking years of history and sending the character in a bold new direction. Peter now had a new supporting cast and it was a brand-new day for Spider-Man.

KEY TO PLATE

1: Civil War: Front Line #2
Spider-Man unmasks his identity.

2: CW #5
Chaos reigns as Spider-Man feels the full force of the war.

3: CW #7
Manhattan turns into one of the biggest warzones in Marvel history, as hero turns against hero.

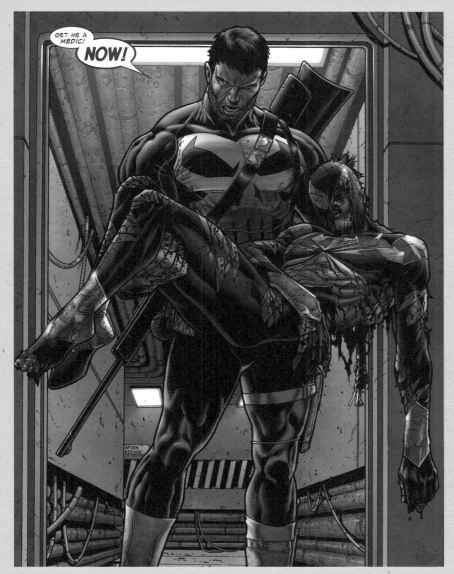

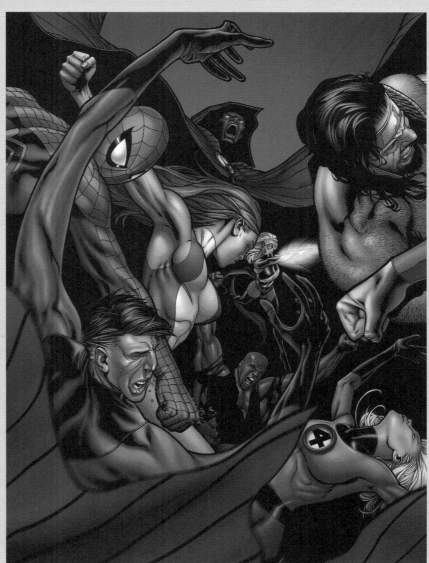

BIG TIME

For once it was time for Peter Parker to catch a break. Despite studying biophysics at Empire State University, Peter had been unable to make science his full-time career – until he got a job at Horizon Labs.

Horizon Labs represents some of the most advanced technology in the world, which in a world that contains Tony Stark, Reed Richards and Hank Pym is really saying something. Made up of seven independent labs, Horizon only has one rule: if you're going to think, think big! Horizon Labs is run by eccentric Max Modell, a science hero of Peter, who strongly believes in giving his staff as much latitude as they need, saying, "It's been my experience that true genius doesn't punch a clock." Modell wasn't sure about Peter at first, but Marla Madison Jameson (Jameson's wife and prominent scientist and robotics expert) vouched for him. Peter soon impressed Modell with his applied use of scientific principles which he'd learned from years of fighting villains as Spider-Man. At first, Peter's job was simple – he had to come up with "the next big thing" every quarter.

Peter was hired as one of Horizon Labs seven lead scientists, known as the Lucky Seven, who were allowed to create whatever they could think of, as long as it was for the betterment of society. These scientists, having no limit to their remit, created inventions ranging from an artificial substitute to vibranium, to a door that opens to the next day! One of the Lucky Seven was revealed to be Michael Morbius, the Living Vampire. This new role subtly altered the character of Spider-Man and how he approached problems. As writer Dan Slott explained at the time, "With Peter's job at Horizon Labs, when Spider-Man has a problem with a villain, Peter Parker [can] come up with a scientific solution and then some peaceful application for his new tech – so he can earn his paycheque. He found a way to have the best of Peter Parker and the best of Spider-Man and have them work in tandem."

The job suited Peter perfectly because he now had his own private lab – a place to work in and store Spider-Man costumes. The level of technology and imagination in Spider-Man costumes improved immediately: Spider-Man now sported an undetectable stealth suit, amazingly strong bulletproof armour and a new Spider-Glider. Peter was able to find a civilian purpose for these brilliant inventions: the technology behind the stealth suit was used to create new noise-cancelling headphones, and the bulletproof Spider-Armour became the basis for a life-saving bike helmet.

Of course, given the old Parker luck, his job did not last for long…

KEY TO PLATE

1: Amazing Spider-Man #648
Is it finally time for Peter Parker to catch a break?

2: ASM #648
Peter has an answer for all of the Lucky Seven's pop quiz questions.

3: ASM #649
Peter finally fulfils Uncle Ben's dream.

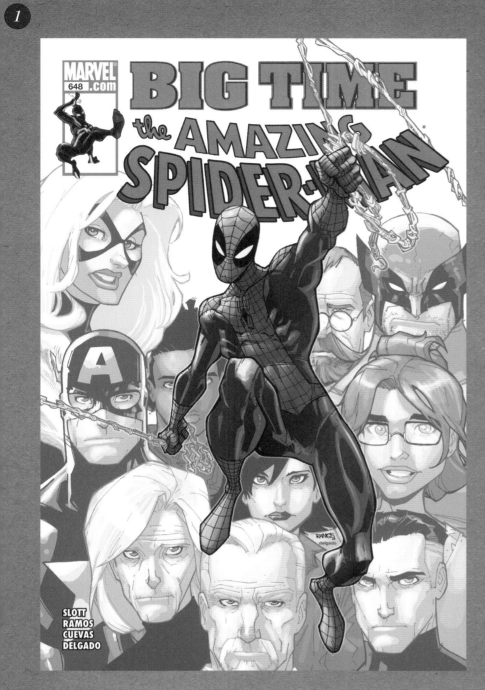

SPIDER-ISLAND

What would happen if everyone in New York had Spider-Man's powers? This is the question asked by the *Spider-Island* event. Spider-Island examines one of Spider-Man's central tenets, "With great power there must also come great responsibility", from another angle. What would happen if everyone had the same great power? Where would Spider-Man's responsibility be then, and who else would accept the same responsibilities as Spider-Man?

Spider-Island drew on threads set up over years of Spider-Man continuity, taking themes from his past with Miles Warren and the Clone Saga, to his present as an Avenger. The plot involved the Jackal and Miles Warren working with the Spider-Queen, a villain who wanted to rule over a world of spider-creatures. The Jackal recruited other spider-powered villains, including everyone from a mutated Kaine to Spider-Woman.

The Spider-Queen's plan worked by connecting New Yorkers to "the Web of Life", a source of spider-related powers across the multiverse. The virus gave everyone spider-powers and was exciting at first, but excitement turned to terror when the virus started to mutate people into horrific spider-like creatures. Reed Richards and Horizon Labs were able to create a vaccine, but this did not work on people who were already infected. New York became a teeming hotspot of spider-powers, and Spider-Man was unable to prove his own identity as he had the same powers as everyone else!

At the climax of the story, Spider-Man uses the Empire State Building as a giant antenna to broadcast a cure to the population of Manhattan. Writer Dan Slott explained that the idea of Spider-Island came from the way that New York is part of the DNA of Spider-Man. "When I was growing up in California, my entire image of New York was from Marvel comics. New York is the extra character in any Spider-Man story…

And a lot of the biggest moments in his life are rooted in New York geography: Gwen Stacy being thrown off the Brooklyn Bridge. [...] In *Spider-Island*, we had Spider-Man and Mary Jane fighting giant spiders on top of the Empire State Building. That's always been their special spot. His meeting place with the Human Torch is the top of the Statue of Liberty. When he pledged that nobody else would ever die while he is Spider-Man, he was overlooking Washington Square Park. Everywhere you look, there's something that links Spider-Man to physical New York."

Spider-Man was given a fitting reward for saving New York – the Empire State building lit up in his iconic red and blue colour scheme!

KEY TO PLATE

1: Amazing Spider-Man #666

If everyone's a Spider-Man then no one is?

2: ASM #667

New York's infestation is complete and Spidey must find a way to reverse it!

3: ASM #666

Not everyone realises that with great power must also come...

SUPERIOR SPIDER-MAN

Doctor Otto Octavius, better known as Doctor Octopus, is perhaps the Spider-Man villain whose origin is closest to Peter Parker. Like Peter, he is a scientific genius who found it difficult to relate to his peers. Like Peter, he gained his powers through a scientific accident, but when Otto's metal arms were fused to his body he shunned society and became a villain, which put him on a collision course with Spider-Man. Being constantly defeated by Spider-Man warped and twisted Doctor Octopus, until he became fixated on proving that he was better than the web-slinger.

When Otto's body started to fail him he hatched his most ambitious plan – to swap consciousness with Spider-Man using a special Octobot. Otto's plan is a success, Peter is trapped in his dying body while Otto takes Peter's body. Just before Peter dies, he floods Otto's mind with his memories, everything that made Peter into Spider-Man. Transformed by these memories, Otto vows to continue Peter's work as Spider-Man, but as a better, Superior Spider-Man.

This was a whole new side to Otto's character that readers had never seen before. As writer Dan Slott put it at the time, "[Otto] wants to be a hero. He's tried being a villain, and he's failed at it miserably. Has he ever had a single plan bear fruit?"[25] He was still the same aloof, condescending and arrogant person that he had always been, but now Octavius had a passion to do good instead of evil.

Otto's mind in Peter's body was something that had never been done before. The Superior Spider-Man had a new suit and new inventions, but had none of the compassion or restraint that defined the friendly neighbourhood Spider-Man. He used spider-bots to patrol the city, and as a matter of pride he took down enemies that Peter had been

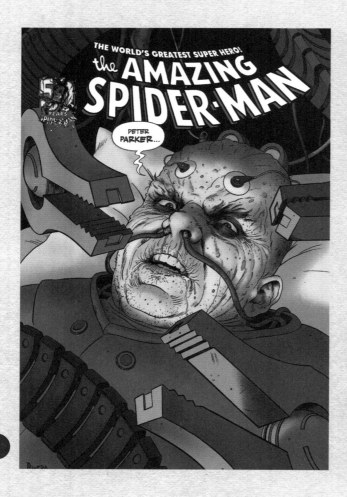

unable to defeat, starting with his old team, the Sinister Six. Octavius wanted the world to see that this was a new, merciless Spider-Man, and publicly executed Massacre, an escaped killer.

Dan clearly loved writing the character: "Sometimes the story just starts happening and you're along for the ride and that's when writing is the most fun. There's that kind of fun with Doc Ock. I just don't know what he's going to do sometimes. Or how he's going to react. The amount of time I spent in Doc Ock's head while doing *Superior Spider-Man* – it was fun! [...] Part of you goes, 'I don't want the ride to end'". [26]

It wasn't enough to be a superior Spider-Man though. Otto wanted to prove that he was better than Peter, so he returned to college to finish his doctorate. He then created Parker Industries, a brilliant multinational rival to Horizon Labs, specialising in advanced technology. Unknown to Otto, Peter's consciousness had been hidden somewhere in the recesses of his mind, gently guiding his decisions. In the end, it was the connections he made as Peter that ended his time as Spider-Man. Otto started a relationship with his tutor, Anna Maria Marconi, and when she was kidnapped by Norman Osborn in his Goblin King persona, Otto realised that the only person who could save her was the real Peter. Otto reluctantly gave Peter back control of his own body, admitting that Peter Parker was the Superior Spider-Man. Back in control of his body Peter found that many things had changed. He had a new suit, a new reputation and even a new company to run! Peter enjoyed running Parker Industries until the company was eventually dissolved as part of a battle with a resurrected Otto.

KEY TO PLATE

1: Amazing Spider-Man #698
A dying Otto Octavius hatches a terrible plan.

2: ASM #698
Trapped in Octavius' dying body, all seems lost for Peter Parker.

3: Superior Spider-Man #1
Otto Octavius in Peter Parker's body was a new, darker Spider-Man with less regard for human life.

4: Superior Spider-Man (2018) #1
Otto added technology to the Spider-Man outfit, but he was consumed by the idea that he had to prove himself superior to Peter.

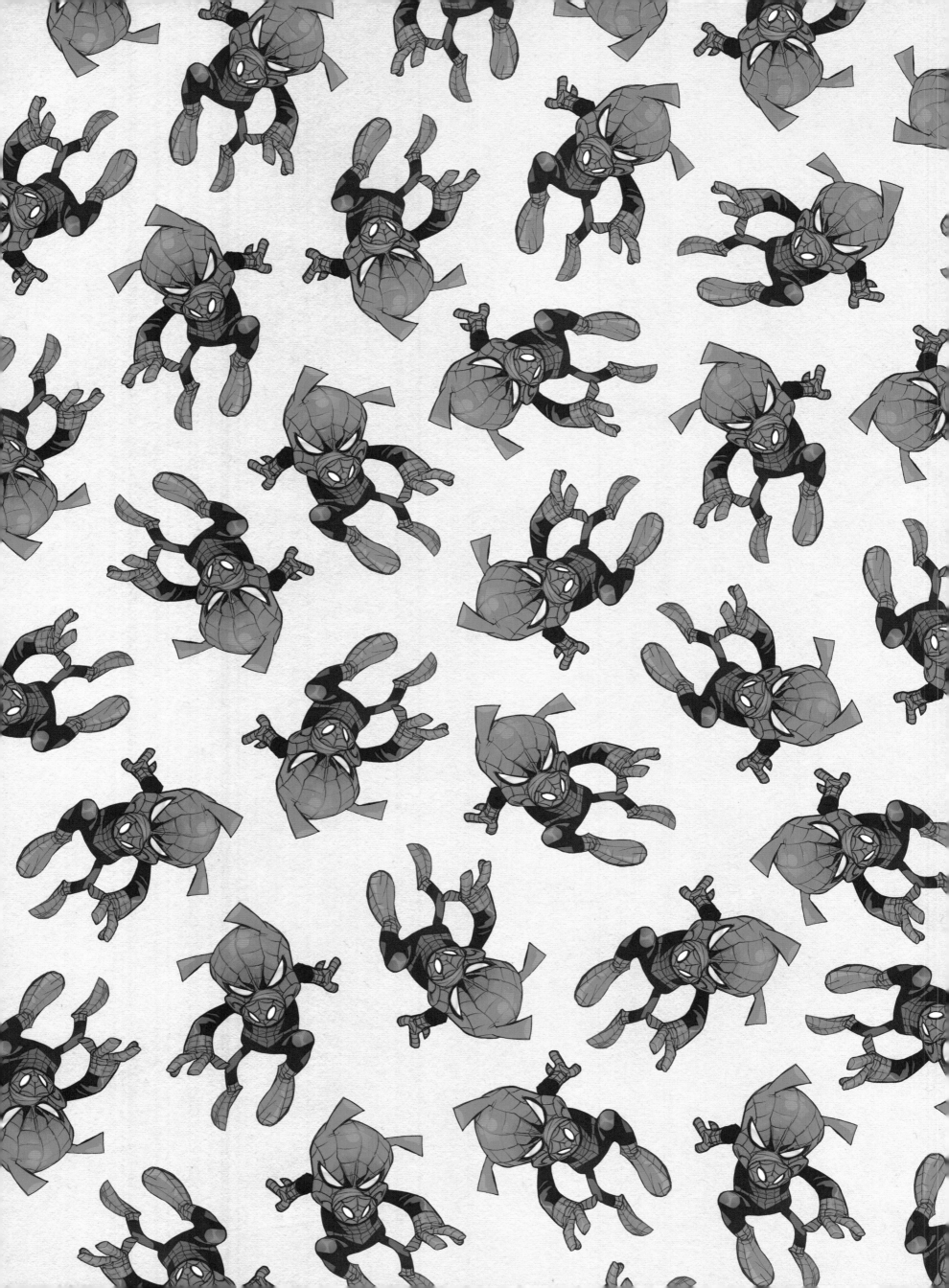

SECTION 5

THE SPIDER-VERSE

Creator Spotlight: Brian Michael Bendis and Sara Pichelli
Spider-Man Miles Morales
Spider-Man 2099
Spider-Woman
Ghost Spider
The Spider-Verse

CREATOR SPOTLIGHT:

BRIAN MICHAEL BENDIS AND SARA PICHELLI

"Most teenagers' lives are so complicated," explained writer Brian Michael Bendis. "That's why so many people relate to the *Spider-Man* franchise – they know that even if they had spider powers, as cool as they are, it wouldn't make life easier. Most people know that if they had powers, it would probably make their life more complicated and more frustrating. People read Spider-Man to have that cathartic experience."[27]

Brian showed readers the complicated, messy and human side of being a teenage super hero, with both Peter Parker and Miles Morales in the *Ultimate Spider-Man* comics. The *Ultimate Comics* universe showed modern, young heroes unencumbered by years of continuity and backstory. The passion for originality didn't come from a desire to

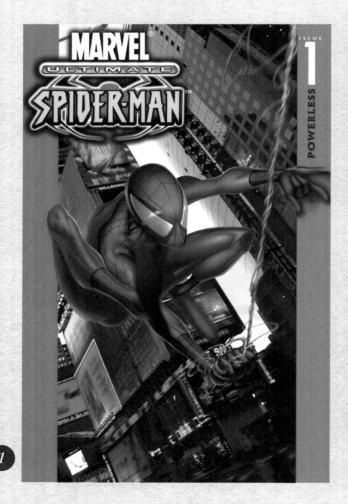

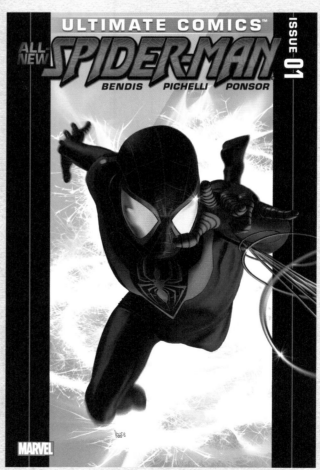

overturn Marvel's existing comics, but from Bendis' love for Marvel. "I was all about the Marvel comics. You name it, I was immersed! I never read a bad [Marvel] comic. They were all equally perfect," Brian laughed.[28]

Part of the success of the book came from the way Brian's dialogue expertly captured the cadence and rhythm of natural conversations. *Ultimate Spider-Man* was able to address the pressures of teenage life, while still telling bold, exciting super hero stories. As artist Sara Pichelli puts it, "He usually creates characters you would like to hang out with or kill with your bare hands. The dialogue is strong and he's able to give life to every character in a page. They're imperfect but believable and multi-faceted."[29]

Another reason for the success of *Ultimate Comics: Spider-Man* is the strong creative partnership between creators Brian and Sara. "The first time I got one of Brian's scripts, it was *Ultimate Spider-Man* before Miles, I almost cried," said Sara. "Half of my reaction was emotions and the other half was anxiety! But I immediately calmed down as I read the first line of the script, he was speaking directly to me, saying hello and explaining why he wanted me on the book. And that made me feel at home right away. I think that's part of the magic of Brian. He's honest, makes his points clear, and at the same time he involves you completely in the creative process, fostering a unique synergy."[30]

"I care a lot about the body language, facial expression and the small details that create a look," explained Sara. "In this way I always try to give my characters a specific personality, of course respecting their own story, and what the writer's intention is."[31]

KEY TO PLATE

1: Ultimate Spider-Man #1
This was a new Peter Parker for the 21st century, but with the classic feel of Spider-Man.

2: Ultimate Comics Spider-Man #1

Miles Morales took over when the Peter Parker of the Ultimate universe died.

3: UCSM #5
Miles is very much his own Spider-Man.

4: Spider-Men #1
History is made as Ultimate Spider-Man Miles Morales meets Peter Parker, the Friendly Neighbourhood Spider-Man!

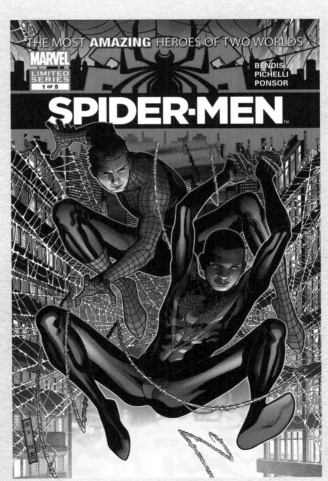

3

4

SPIDER-MAN MILES MORALES

The idea behind the Ultimate Marvel comics line, launched in the year 2000, was a bold but simple one. As Bill Jemas, president of Marvel at the time, put it, "Marvel's greatest teen characters – Spidey and the X-Men – started as teenagers in the 1960s and won the hearts of a generation of teens. [...] The way to win new, younger readers [...] would be to recast them as teenagers."[32] This exciting new universe was unencumbered by Marvel continuity and allowed writers to tell relevant new stories about modern teens.

The new Peter Parker of *Ultimate Spider-Man* had the same origin story as the main Marvel Universe version, but with the added complications of modern life. A computer-literate and tech-savvy Peter could use the worldwide web to catch criminals as well as any webs he spun. The Ultimate Universe Peter grew to become a great and inspiring teenage super hero. And then he died in a battle with the Green Goblin of Ultimate Universe.

But that wasn't the end of Ultimate Spider-Man: enter Miles Morales. Miles Morales, a teenager who had been following Peter's career, gained spider-powers from a different genetically altered spider.

Writer Brian Michael Bendis and artist Sara Pichelli thought carefully about how to make Miles Morales a fully rounded character. Miles Morales is the son of an African American father and a Puerto Rican mother, giving him a very different perspective on being a super hero. Unlike Peter, he has active, involved parents and a trusted circle of close friends. The anxieties and challenges of Miles Morales are different from Peter's, but also echo the original remit of *Ultimate Comics* — teenage heroes with teenage problems. Once again, the beauty of all the Spider-Man costumes is that Spidey could be anyone under the mask.

Though he started in the Ultimate Universe, Miles Morales jumped to the main Marvel Universe after the Multiverse-contracting event of Secret Wars. Miles Morales has become a key part of the Marvel Universe, joining teen super hero group the Champions, while becoming close friends with Ms Marvel, Kamala Khan. As Sara puts it, "Miles slowly earned the readers' affection [as he was revealed] to be a complex and unique character, strong enough to be finally included in a bigger picture."[33]

"Being part of the creation of Miles Morales is the highest point in my career," said Sara. "It was an ideal condition for an artist like me who loves telling stories and designing characters: I was able to merge [these] two passions and at the same time work on one of the most beloved icons, Spider-Man."[34]

Miles Morales and Peter Parker are both Spider-Man, but have come to represent different parts of the Spider-Man myth. "Miles [is] the Spider-Man that is trying desperately to balance his life as a high school student and his super hero career," explains Bendis. "He [is] the character that is wrestling with power and responsibility in a very raw way."[35]

KEY TO PLATE

1: Miles Morales: The Ultimate Spider-Man #1

Miles Morales returns with a new outlook on life.

SPIDER-MAN 2099

In 1992, Marvel launched the *Marvel 2099* line of comics, with exciting new versions of familiar heroes over 100 years into a dystopian future. Writer Peter David and artist Rick Leonardi introduced Spider-Man 2099 and Miguel O'Hara, a scientist who had his genetic code rewritten with spider DNA. Navigating an oppressive futurescape ruled by giant corporations while hiding spider-powers isn't easy, and so Miguel donned a spare Day of the Dead costume, becoming an updated Spider-Man in the process.

Peter David wanted to make Miguel (named after Peter David's friend, actor Miguel Ferrer) as tonally different from Peter Parker as possible, purposefully taking the contrary directions from the choices made by Stan Lee and Steve Ditko when they created Spider-Man. "If we wanted to do a series starring a character with the same psychological profile, background, and powers we would've done the original Spider-Man," explained Peter David. "Everywhere the original Spidey zigs, Spider-Man 2099 zags."[36] Peter was an only child, Miguel had a brother. Peter was an awkward teenager but Miguel was in his 20s and had a fiancée. Instead of an elderly, doting Aunt May, Miguel has a beautiful hologramatic AI personal assistant. Lyla (an acronym of LYrate Lifeform Approximation) was Miguel's confidante, friend and sidekick, and despite being a computer program, Lyla is the only person that Miguel trusts.

As well as Spider-Man 2099, the 2099 universe launched with Punisher 2099, Doom 2099 and a new hero, Ravage 2099, created by Stan. This was a bleak and suffocating future, grown in the shadow of civil war between humans and mutants, ruled by oligarchic regimes. The editor of the *Marvel 2099* line, Joey Cavalieri, was keen to keep the inherent social commentary, saying, "Like a lot of good science fiction, it really turns out to be a comment on the way we, as individuals, live now in our society. Most science fiction is a reaction to the fears that we have about what the future will be like. And I think these comics address this really well. [...] What these series do is take our problems, push them to the absolute max, and then present people who are thrust into the position of doing something about these problems."[37]

KEY TO PLATE

1: Spider-Man 2099 #1
Introducing the new Spider-Man for the year 2099.

2: Spider-Man 2099 (2015) #1
Artist Will Sliney gave Miguel O'Hara a bold new look.

3: SP 2099 (2015) #1
Miguel O'Hara has had many adventures through time. For a long time he was stuck in the present day, where he became friends with Peter.

4: SP 2099 #1
New York is a different place in the year 2099, but there will always be a Spider-Man!

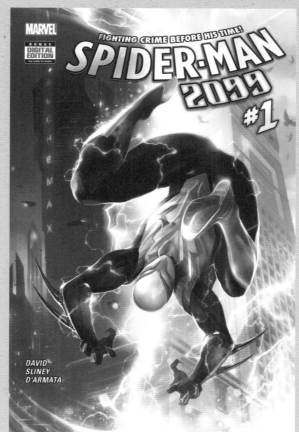

SPIDER-WOMAN

Spider-Woman first appeared in *Marvel Spotlight #32* in 1977. Created by Archie Goodwin and Sal Buscema, with a costume design by Marie Severin, Spider-Woman was Jessica Drew, a super-powered secret agent who had been deceived by terrorist organisation Hydra into attacking Nick Fury and law-enforcement agency S.H.I.E.L.D. Spider-Man was purposefully nowhere in the issue, so that Spider-Woman could establish her own identity.

Much like Spider-Man, Spider-Woman was unexpectedly popular after her first appearance and she was given her own ongoing series in April 1978. Her costume was altered slightly to show her long hair, and her origin story was tweaked so that it was no longer implied that she was a spider that had been mutated into a human being. Jessica got her spider-powers from a spider serum given to her by her scientist father to cure radiation poisoning when she was a child.

Boasting that "To know her is to fear her", *Spider-Woman #1* is a dark, paranoid comic, featuring much of the nervous tension that categorised the Stan and Steve years of *Spider-Man*, but set against an espionage backdrop. Jessica has relocated to London, but she is not welcome there. "There she is again. God, she makes my skin crawl," mutters Jessica's neighbour as she walks past. Like Peter Parker, Jessica is an outcast, but she doesn't share his wild moments of youthful optimism. *Spider-Woman* ran for 50 issues and ended with Jessica seemingly dying in a climactic battle with her nemesis Morgan le Fay. The character soon returned, however, and briefly joined the Avengers.

Other characters have taken the name Spider-Woman, including Julia Carpenter, an Avenger who wore a costume similar to Spider-Man's black outfit. For a while, Mattie Franklin, a super powered Spider-Man fan, also took the name Spider-Woman and fought crime with help from Jessica and Madame Web. Jessica became a member of the Avengers in 2005's *New Avengers*, joining Spider-Man on the team. However, this character was revealed in 2009 to be a shapeshifting Skrull imposter, the Queen of the Skrulls, who was leading an invasion of Earth. The real Jessica returned to a life of crime-fighting shortly after the failed Skrull attack.

KEY TO PLATE

1: Marvel Spotlight #32
The world is introduced to a new super hero.

2: The Spider-Woman #1
Jessica Drew's comic was a dark tale of espionage.

3: Spider-Woman (2015) #1
Jessica Drew returned as a private investigator, a super hero and a mum to be!

4: Spider-Woman (1993) #1
Other characters have taken the name Spider-Woman.

5: Spider-Woman Origin #5
The source of Jessica Drew's powers and her parents' links to Hydra were revealed in this 2005 miniseries.

SPIDER-WOMAN #1

HOPELESS
RODRIGUEZ
LOPEZ

MARVEL

GHOST SPIDER

The death of Gwen Stacy is one of the pivotal moments in Peter Parker's life; his failure to save her has informed every decision he made ever since. Except, what if Gwen had got spider-powers and Peter had died? In this universe (Earth-65), high school student Gwen was bitten by a radioactive spider and takes the identity of Spider-Woman. Her friend, Peter, injects himself with a formula that turns him into a mutant lizard and dies in a battle with Spider-Woman. Not only does Gwen feel the guilt of Peter's death, but Spider-Woman is branded a public menace and is hunted by her own father, NYPD Captain George Stacy.

Gwen's Earth is a slightly twisted reflection of the main Marvel universe, with characters taking different roles: Frank Castle (the Punisher) is a police officer, while Matt Murdock (Daredevil) is the Kingpin of Crime.

The character initially appeared in *Edge of Spider-Verse #2* and was a huge hit with fans. *Spider-Gwen* comics followed (with Gwen later taking the super hero name Ghost Spider), showing the different powers and responsibilities of Gwen's world. Robbi Rodriguez's designs for Gwen's iconic costume intentionally set her apart from traditional Marvel colour palettes, giving her a neon, neo-noir feel. The minimalist use of colour, along with the mask and hoodie, allowed the character to keep a level of mystery, while at the same time linking her to Spider-Man. "We get to interpret the character of Gwen in this new light," said Robbi. "We get to punk her out a bit, and make her a kind of heroine that […] female readers can relate with."[38]

This Gwen is a creative, free-spirited teenager, with a supportive group of friends, but just like Spider-Man, the weight of spider-powers hangs heavy on her. Gwen is the drummer in the rock group The Mary Janes, along with her universe's Mary Jane Watson, Glory Grant and Betty Brant, but the duties of being a super hero often clash with the demands of being in a band. "Though many of the elements of her day-to-day life are the same as the classic version of the character, this Gwen is a little more curious about, and at the same time in conflict with, the world around her," says creator Jason Latour. "Some of it stems from struggling with what having her powers means, but it's just as much about trying to figure out what she wants out of her civilian life. Gwen's in a band, she wants to be an artist. But how practical or responsible is that when suddenly you can lift cars and stick to walls?"[39]

KEY TO PLATE

1: Spider-Gwen: Ghost Spider #1
Gwen discovers her new-found freedom.

2: Edge of Spider-Verse #2
Gwen's initial appearance in the Spider comicbookdom.

3: Spider-Gwen #1
Spider-Gwen gets her very own series.

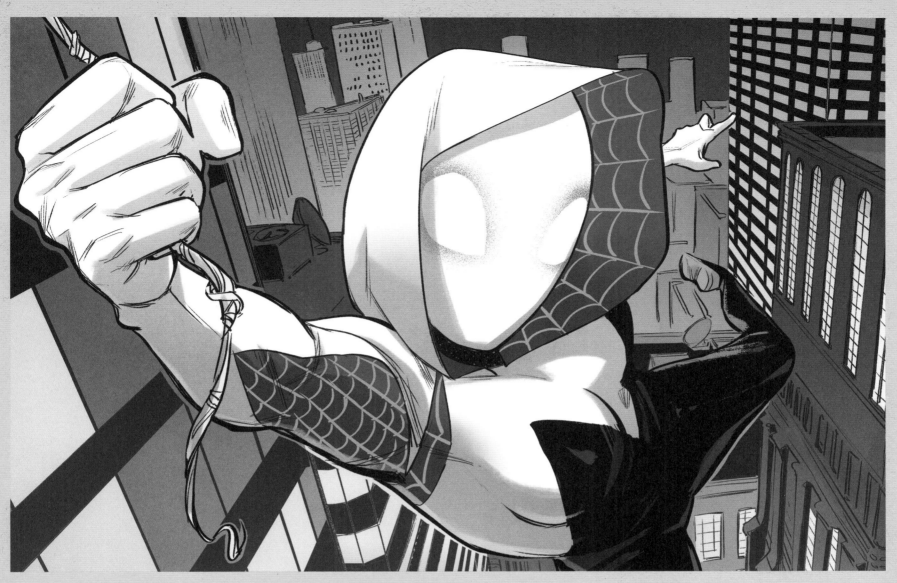

THE SPIDER-VERSE

The idea for the Multiverse-spanning *Spider-Verse* event came from writer Dan Slott's work outside of comics. "I worked on a Spider-Man video game called *Spider-Man: Shattered Dimensions* and they wanted to have four Spider-Men: Spider-Man, Spider-Man Noir, Ultimate Spider-Man and Spider-Man 2099. They were all going to get together and have this big adventure. [...] I called up my editor and said, 'They're doing this game, and it's amazing with all the different Spider-Men, but it's bugging me that they can't interact with each other. We should do this in the comic, but instead of four Spider-Men, we should do every Spider-Man ever!'"[40]

Peter Parker, the original Spider-Man created by Stan Lee and Steve Ditko, lives in one universe that is part of a giant web of alternate universes – a multiverse. The main Marvel Universe is Earth-616, but there are many more universes and many more Spider-heroes.

The 2014 Spider-Verse storyline is perhaps the most ambitious and far-reaching event in Spider-Man's history. The idea was simple – bring together nearly every single spider-powered individual as part of a universe-spanning battle with the psychic vampire Morlun, and his evil family, the Inheritors. "The sheer scope of this event and the amount of Spider-Characters in it are mind-boggling," shared editor Nick Lowe. "But what's crazy is that Dan Slott and Olivier [Copiel] have been able to squeeze everything but still have a story that has heart and truly counts."[41]

Different versions of Spider-Man have been retold in many different settings over the years. *Spider-Man Noir* was part of the *Marvel Noir* line of comics launched in 2009, which showcased dark, Depression-era versions of Marvel heroes. The Peter Parker in *Spider-Man Noir* fought gangland boss Norman Osborn in the 1930s from the shadows, clad in his trademark trench coat and fedora.

Other versions of Spider-Man varied wildly in tone. First introduced in 1983's *Marvel Tails Starring Peter Porker, the Spectacular Spider-Ham*, Peter Porker is a talking pig who lives in a universe of anthropomorphic animals. Everything in Porker's universe is an animal version of the Marvel Universe; he works for the J. Jonah Jackal at the *Daily Beagle* and teams up with super heroes Captain Ameri-cat, Iron Mouse and Croctor Strange, while fighting villains such as Ducktor Doom and Kangaroo the Conqueror.

Peter is not, of course, the only spider-powered super hero even on Earth-616. Cindy

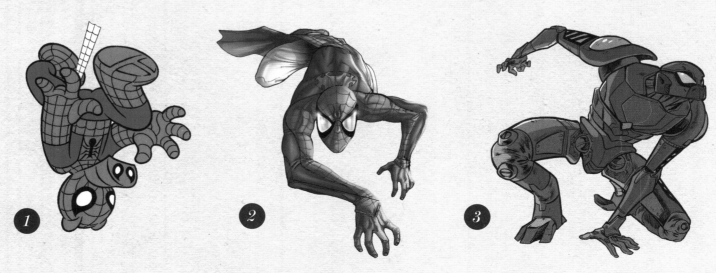

Moon was bitten by the same radioactive spider as Parker, but instead of becoming a super hero she was hidden away for her own protection. When she was freed by Spider-Man she became the super hero Silk. She has many of the same powers as Spidey but can also produce organic webbing from her fingertips.

The Spider-Verse was bigger than fans had dared hope. Not only did it include Parker, Miles Morales, Spider-Man 2099, Spider-Man Noir, Kaine, the Scarlet Spider, Pavitr Prabhakar (a Spider-Man from India) and the Superior Spider-Man, but it also brought in Spider-Men from other mediums, including an animated Spider-Man and video game Spider-Man.

Spider-powered characters Spider-Woman, Silk and Ghost Spider were joined by multiple Spider-Women: May "Mayday" Parker (the daughter of Peter Parker and Mary Jane Watson from an alternate future) and Anya Corazon, a young hero who got her powers from a spider tattoo.

New exciting versions of Spider-Man were created especially for the event; Spider-UK is Billy Braddock, upstanding member of the Captain Britain Corps. Spider-Punk is Hobie Brown, a rebellious New York teenager. Spiders-Man is actually thousands of radioactive spiders who think they are Peter Parker. Peni Parker, created by Gerard Way and Jake Wyatt, is a high school student, who powers a mech called SP//dr which is also partially controlled by a radioactive spider. Spider-Ma'am comes from a universe where Aunt May was bitten by the radioactive spider instead of Peter Parker.

KEY TO PLATE

1: Peter Porker

2: Spider-Man Pavitr Prabhakar

3: Peni Parker

4: Spider-Man Noir

5: Spider-Girl

6: Cindy Moon AKA Silk

7: Spider-Ma'am

8: Spider-Punk

9: Cosmic Spider-Man

Why Spider-Man?

Why is Spider-Man such an incredibly popular character? What is it about Peter Parker that still excites readers 60 years after the character was first introduced?

Part of his enduring appeal is due to the fact that anyone could be behind the mask, but it's also because we can project so many of our own hopes, fears and aspirations onto Spider-Man. The broad canvas of the character means that Spider-Man can be anything from a wise-cracking goof to a tortured vigilante, often in the space of a few pages. Spider-Man can be a detective, a scientist, a concerned nephew, a romantic lead, a star student, a mentor, a loner, one of the most popular people in New York and everything in between. There are few super heroes who can pull off being an Avenger and a friendly neighbourhood Spider-Man at the same time.

Being part of the Marvel Universe means that Spider-Man has a wide range of heroes to bounce off, like Iron Man, Captain America and the Hulk. In the same way, Peter Parker is broadened and sharpened by a supporting cast of characters. Aunt May shows us Peter's personal responsibility, Mary Jane unveils his sensitive side, while J. Jonah Jameson demonstrates the cost of Peter's double life. Spider-Man has a deeper bench of villains than pretty much any other hero, and part of the joy of the character is seeing an underdog face, and beat, impossible odds.

Spider-Man may be versatile, but he is also deep. Stan Lee and Steve Ditko set up a specific moral universe for Peter Parker. While Spider-Man's circumstances have changed over the years, his personal code of ethics has not. Peter Parker may have the proportional strength and speed of a spider, but his real super power is being able to find the strength to always do the right thing, no matter the cost. Why is Spider-Man so popular? He has been a moral compass for generations, a character that does not compromise on his ethics. It's no accident that Spider-Man first became popular in the second half of the 20th century, in an age of moral ambiguity and compromised role models. He stands for something more while being honest and true.

Why Spider-Man? Because he is an example to us all.

SPIDER-MAN MUSEUM

SECTION 6

LIBRARY

Index
References

INDEX

REFERENCES

1   Marvel Age #114, page 6
2   Marvel Masterworks Amazing Spider-
     Man Volume 1, introduction
3   Marvel Masterworks Amazing Spider-
     Man Volume 1, introduction
4   Marvel Age #111, page 16
5   Marvel Age #111, page 8
6   Marvel Masterworks Amazing Spider-
     Man Volume 6, introduction
7   Marvel.com interview, 13 January 2022
8   Marvel.com interview, 13 January 2022
9   Marvel Masterworks Amazing Spider-
     Man Volume 2, introduction
10   Marvel Masterworks Amazing Spider-
     Man Volume 5, introduction
11   Marvel Masterworks Amazing Spider-
     Man Volume 2, introduction
12   Comics Creators on Spider-Man, page
     142
13   Marvel Age #114, page 8
14   Marvel: Five Fabulous Decades of the
     World's Greatest Comics, page 222
15   Comics Creators on Spider-Man, page
     142
16   Marvel Masterworks Amazing Spider-
     Man Volume 2, introduction
17   Marvel Masterworks Amazing Spider-
     Man Volume 5, introduction
18   Marvel Masterworks Amazing Spider-
     Man Volume 13, introduction
19   Marvel Masterworks Amazing Spider-

Man Volume 13, introduction
20   Spider-Man: The Saga of the Alien
     Costume, introduction
21   Marvel Age #114, page 9
22   Amazing Spider-Man #801, page 21
23   Marvel.com interview, 22 March 2017
24   Marvel.com interview, 18 January 2018
25   Marvel.com interview, 22 March 2017
26   Marvel.com interview, 22 March 2017
27   Marvel.com interview, 12 September,
     2017
28   Ultimate Spider-Man Volume 1,
     afterword
29   Marvel.com interview, 22 June, 2015
30   Marvel.com interview, 29 May, 2014
31   Marvel.com interview, 29 May, 2014
32   Marvel Age #114, page 10
33   Marvel Age #117, page 15
34   Ultimate Spider-Man Hardcover,
     Volume 1
35   Marvel.com interview, 22 June, 2015
36   Marvel.com interview, 29 May, 2014
37   Marvel.com interview, 22 June, 2015
38   Marvel.com interview, 10 June, 2014
39   Marvel.com interview, 10 June, 2014
40   Marvel's Declassified, S1: EP9 Spider-
     Verse Secrets Revealed
41   Marvel.com interview, 27 October,
     2014